WELCOME TO
YOUR MINISTRY

WELCOME TO YOUR MINISTRY

LAY ACTION MINISTRY PROGRAM
7200 E. DRY CREEK ROAD, SUITE D-202
ENGLEWOOD, CO 80112

Scripture quotations, unless otherwise noted, are taken from the Holy Bible: New International Version, © 1973, 1978, 1984 by the International Bible Society, used by permission of Zondervan Bible Publishers.

93 92 91 90 89   5   4   3   2

David C. Cook Publishing Co.
850 North Grove Avenue
Elgin, IL 60120
Printed in U.S.A.

Editor: Gary Wilde
Designer: Chris Patchel
Cover: Lois Rosio Sprague

ISBN: 0-89191-515-x
Library of Congress Catalog Number: 86-72601

TABLE OF
CONTENTS

LAY ACTION
MINISTRY PROGRAM

LAMP courses are based on the HEAD, HEART, and HANDS approach to learning. HEAD represents Bible *content* that you want to know. HEART represents your *personal application* of the truth. HANDS refers to the LAMP goal of preparing you to *use course content in the lives of other people*—imparting to others what you have learned (see II Tim. 2:2).

Welcome to Your Ministry can be the finest study experience of your life. If you diligently study each lesson, this course can transform your understanding of ministry, help you understand your ministry gifts, and encourage you to launch into a ministry for Christ.

Course Requirements

This course is for every Christian who is willing to put forth the effort in personal study. But we want you to know "up front" what it is going to cost you in terms of time and commitment. *It is going to cost you a good hour of home study for each lesson*. Make every effort to spend this much time as a minimum requirement.

How to Use This Course

Though you may complete the course by yourself, you will normally be preparing for a weekly group meeting. In this meeting you will be an active participant because of your personal study. One lesson is to be completed each week, prior to coming to the weekly group meeting.

The weekly group meeting for this course features a discussion of the lesson that you have studied during the week. It also includes other elements to encourage group life, and to guide group members toward personal application of the material. The meeting, planned for at least a full hour, should be led by a person who enjoys leading discussions and helping people learn. The study leader will study the lesson in the same way as anyone else in the group. In addition, a **Leader's Guide** is available, with specific suggestions for conducting each weekly group meeting. This **Leader's Guide** can be obtained from:

DAVID C. COOK PUBLISHING CO.
850 NORTH GROVE AVENUE
ELGIN, IL 60120

or:

LAY ACTION MINISTRY PROGRAM, INC.
7200 E. DRY CREEK ROAD, SUITE D-202
ENGLEWOOD, CO 80112

GOD'S OBJECTIVES
FOR LIFE

Go to a graveyard outside Lincoln, Kansas, and you'll see an unusual group of gravestones. They were erected by a man named Davis. When you delve into his personal history, you discover that he began working as a lowly hired hand. Over the years, though, by sheer determination and extreme frugality, he amassed a wallet-bulging fortune. You also find out that Mr. Davis's preoccupation with wealth resulted in a neglect of people. Apparently, he had few friends. He was even emotionally distant from his wife's family, who felt that she had married beneath her dignity. Their attitude embittered him. He vowed never to leave his relatives a penny.

When his wife died, Davis hired a sculptor to design an elaborate monument in her memory. The monument consisted of a love seat showing Mr. Davis and his wife sitting together. The result so pleased him that he paid for another statue—this one showing him kneeling at his wife's grave, placing a wreath on it. That was followed by a third monument—showing his wife kneeling at his future gravesite. His monument-building binge continued until he'd spent more than a quarter of a million dollars!

He was often approached about contributing financial aid to worthwhile projects in the town or church. But he rarely gave to them. Most of his small fortune was invested in gravestones. At 92, Mr. Davis died—a sour-hearted resident of the poorhouse.

Decades later, as you saunter through the graveyard, you notice an ironic fact: each monument he commissioned is slowly sinking into the Kansas soil, a victim of neglect, vandalism, and time. Inevitably, these temporal objects will follow him into the grave.

God's Objectives

We're instinctively repelled by such an eccentric expenditure of time and money. "What a waste!" we're prone to cry. We think of loftier, less selfish pursuits that could have enhanced the lives of countless people.

Yet Mr. Davis's strange investments may still reap dividends—if we let the story of his life serve as a stimulus for evaluating our own lives. When is the last time you evaluated how you are investing your life? Consider these soul-jarring questions:

- What are *God's* objectives for my life?
- To what extent am I investing my life and God-given resources in *eternal*, rather than just *temporal*, matters?
- What "monuments" do I want to leave behind when I die?

How we answer such questions is crucial—if we want to avoid Mr. Davis's mistake. That's why the initial lesson in this *Welcome to Your Ministry* course is titled "God's Objectives for Life." No matter what vocation God has called us to, we must latch onto His purposes for life on planet Earth. Unless we do, and adjust our priorities accordingly, we can't fulfill the potential He has implanted within each of us. We are prone to elevate our own objectives above His, using entirely different criteria to determine what it means to be a success in life.

This initial lesson doesn't deal with the issue of guidance, or God's specific, individualized will for your life. Which job offer you accept, whom you marry, etc., are

10

matters that require prayerful deliberation. But they are outside the scope of this lesson. Instead, Lesson 1 puts the spotlight on the broad, overarching objectives that are the same for everyone. If Mr. Davis had ordered his life and resources according to the following objectives, he would have left more marks on lives, and fewer on marble.

First Things First

1. The following verses reveal God's primary objectives for your life. Read them carefully, and list every word or phrase from these verses that reflect the desire of God's heart in relation to humanity.

John 3:16, 17 _____

_____

John 17:3 _____

_____

II Timothy 2:1-6 _____

_____

II Peter 3:9 _____

_____

2. What initiative, or work, on God's part was required before this objective could be fulfilled? (To answer this, pick out specific words or phrases from the verses in exercise #1 that show what God the Father or Jesus Christ has done for us. Then, for further clarification, read Romans 5:6-8.)

_____

_____

_____

3. Look at John 3:16, 17 and II Peter 3:9 again. Also examine Romans 10:9, 10. What words or phrases from

these verses reveal how we should respond to God's initiative?

_____

_____

_____

4. What one word best summarizes this ultimate objective for your life?

_____

Sin has driven a wedge between every human being and God. But Jesus' death and resurrection has removed that wedge. If we believe in the need for Christ's sacrifice, and receive Him as Savior, we are no longer in a cut-off-from-God state. We become reconciled with our Maker. This is salvation—a new relationship with God. Before God's other purposes for our lives can be fulfilled, we must enter into this personal relationship with Him. Conversion is the entrance point for that ongoing relationship. It is the initial giving ourselves over to Christ through faith. Whether it is a dramatic event (like the conversion of Paul, for instance) or a more quiet coming to faith, conversion marks the entrance into eternal life, and into the community of God's people, the Church.

Have *you* accepted God's gift of salvation? If so, pause and thank Him now for the gift of eternal life. If not, perhaps God is preparing your heart to receive Christ right now. Consider the words of Jesus: "What good is it for a man to gain the whole world, yet forfeit his soul?" (Mk. 8:36). To put it another way, *there is no failure as disastrous as success without God!*

Born to Grow

Jay Kesler, former President of Youth for Christ U.S.A., wrote a column in *Campus Life* magazine in which he points to God's second objective for your life:

"When you're introduced to someone, you may go away with goose pimples of excitement, or you may feel 'so what?' But regardless of your feelings, you don't 'know' that person . . . not yet, anyway. It's the same with Christ. If you've accepted Him into your life, you've got the introduction, but there is a lot of growing to do in your relationship."

1. What one word from this statement by Kesler summarizes God's desire for every person after conversion?

---

2. In his church-planting ministry, the apostle Paul wasn't content with merely the conversion of others. What else did he desire? (Read Col. 1:28 and jot down your answer.)

---

3. Now put Romans 8:29; Galatians 4:19; and Ephesians 4:14, 15 under your mental microscope. In what other ways did Paul describe this overarching objective that God has for every believer?

Just as one's wedding day is only the start of an ongoing commitment to another person, the conversion experience is the inauguration ceremony to a life-long relationship with Christ. God's ultimate goal for every believer includes intimacy with Christ, which produces maturity. In the spheres of home, work, leisure activities—you name it—He wants the qualities of Jesus Christ to surface. However, growth to maturity isn't an automatic benefit distributed to every Christian. It is a supernatural goal that requires daily, grace-motivated effort to tap into the Lord's resources for godliness. On a day-by-day basis, we make choices that determine whether we will remain a spiritual infant, or edge closer to spiritual adulthood.

4. Pause for a moment of reflection. Compare your current spiritual state with where you were spiritually one year ago. What seeds of growth have sprouted up during the past twelve months? (Describe these evidences below, and say a prayer of thanksgiving for each.)

_____

_____

_____

_____

_____

_____

On Purpose

Many people have the misconception that Christianity is boring. They think that all the real action is in the world of business, or the arena of sports, or in some sort of freewheeling, unconventional life-style. Their misconception, though, shows how little they know about Scripture. Some of the most hair-raising adventures ever recorded are found in the Bible. Few contemporary personalities lead lives as daring and zestful as folks like Abraham, David, Paul, and Peter.

The exciting news is that _no believer in the will of God leads a boring existence._ No siree! That's because God's purpose for every believer includes participation in His grand work in the world. Every Christian is to be involved in the adventure of serving the Lord, of making an impact for Him in his or her sphere of influence. When it's lived authentically, Christianity is the farthest thing from boredom!

Crack open your Bible to John 15:5, 8, 16; II Corinthians 5:17-20; and I Peter 2:9, 10. What phrases from

14

these verses emphasize that ministry is one of God's ultimate purposes for our lives?

_____

_____

_____

_____

_____

_____

Imagine—God wants to change the complexion of the world and redirect the course of human lives through you! Even Christians who aren't called to earn their living in some form of pastoral ministry—and that's the vast majority—are called into God's service. (The Biblical roots of this concept will be unearthed in future lessons of this course. Right now, we're merely introducing it in correlation with the other fundamental objectives that God has for your life.)

Let's retrace our steps for a minute. In this initial lesson, you've learned that God has at least three foundational objectives for your life. These are objectives that depend upon God's initiative and resources for fulfillment, but which we can choose to adopt or to ignore.

He wants you to . . .
• Know Christ personally (experience a Person)
• Grow to maturity (experience a Process)
• Serve Him regularly (experience a Purpose)

Only persons committed to these ultimate objectives reach their full potential. Such individuals view their earthly existence from the perspective of eternity—and they want as many other persons as possible to choose the same objectives.

Remember Mr. Davis, who purchased a bevy of gravestones? What he selected as life objectives are now decaying and sinking into the Kansas soil. But your life investments can last forever!

The Receiving End

The theme of this course is participation in ministry. Such participation is a by-product of your salvation experience and growth in Christlikeness. To apply this first lesson, think of lay ministries that have helped you personally.

Think of a time when the Lord used another lay person to contribute to your spiritual life. This Christian brother or sister may have aided you through an official role in the church, such as elder or Sunday school teacher. Perhaps he or she ministered to you informally through counseling, encouragement, hospitality, or provision of a material need.

Before the next meeting of your study group, write this person a brief thank-you note. Inform this person of the specific difference God made in your life through his or her input. Also, describe your involvement in this course. Tell this person you want to have the kind of impact in others' lives that he or she has had on yours! In addition, ask this person to pray for you at least once each week throughout the duration of this course. Prayer support can enable you to get the most from the workbook exercises and group meetings.

2

GOD'S PLAN
FOR THE CHURCH

According to *Webster's New Collegiate Dictionary,* the term "agency" refers to "a person or thing through which power is exerted or an end is achieved." That's what the Church is! A divinely ordained channel through which God's power moves to achieve His purposes. Individuals cannot isolate themselves from a local church and still fulfill their God-intended roles in ministry.

What Is the Church?

In Lesson 1, we learned that how we invest our lives—time, energies, abilities—should be shaped by God's objectives for His people. We are successful in God's eyes if we have a personal relationship with Him (salvation), if we're committed to a lifelong process of maturing in Christ, and if we're actively participating in His work in the world. Only by riveting this perspective deeply into our consciousness can we avoid being caught in the pythonic grip of an earthly, or temporal, value system.

Lessons 2 and 3 add a different perspective to our involvement in ministry. God's primary agency for accomplishing His work in the world is the local church. These lessons sketch God's plan for the church and its leadership. Whether our ministries are inside or outside the formal program of a church, it is essential to view the church as a framework, or foundation, for individual involvement in God's redemptive plan.

Since the church is that important, let's gain at least a skeletal understanding of what the New Testament says about it.

When you hear or see the word "church" what immediately pops into your mind? Write your associations here:

_____

_____

_____

The term conjures up a lot of mental images: towering steeples, stained-glass windows, denominational hierarchies, particular forms of church government or modes of baptism. And to be sure, what people associate with the word is influenced by both negative and positive past experiences. Yet it is Scripture—not personal experience—that accurately defines the church.

The Greek word for "church," *ekklesia*, literally means "a called-out group or assembly." The word is found 115 times in the New Testament. The term isn't always used in a religious sense, though. In Acts 19:39, the word refers to a lawful assembly that could be summoned to determine civic policy. Applied to Christians, the Church refers to those who have been "called out" for salvation through Jesus Christ's work on the cross.

More specifically, in the New Testament the concept of "church" is used two ways:

1. THE UNIVERSAL CHURCH. The Church is universal in that it includes all true believers in every place, plus those who have died as well as those still living. Every person whom the Lord has ever saved is part of the universal Church. At least 12 references to "church" in the New Testament are used this way.

2. THE LOCAL CHURCH. A local church is a visible, concrete cell of the universal Church. In his *Systematic*

Theology, A. H. Strong puts it this way: "The individual church may be defined as that smaller company of regenerate persons who, in any given community, unite themselves voluntarily in accordance with Christ's laws, for the purpose of securing the complete establishment of His Kingdom in themselves and in the world."

In the New Testament, the term "church" refers to local bodies of believers at least 90 times. Thus the term predominantly refers to the local, visible, organized church.

a. Look up the following verses and indicate which refers to the local church and which to the universal Church:

Ephesians 1:22, 23 _____

I Corinthians 1:1, 2 _____

Ephesians 5:24, 25 _____

Acts 13:1 _____

b. Next, before we pinpoint God's goals for the church, think through some practical implications of what we've already covered. Now that we've defined what the church is, jot down a couple of things the church IS NOT. (Your responses should capture misconceptions of, or shallow associations people make with, the term "church.")

_____

_____

_____

_____

c. You've learned that *ekklesia* refers to all true Christians as well as to people in an organized, local assembly. Whereas Scripture points to the universal Church 12 times, there are at least 90 references to local assemblies. What are some practical implications of these two definitions and the related statistics?

_____

_____

_____

_____

Why Does the Church Exist?

Think for a minute about your local church's calendar of activities. What ongoing agencies and programs dot the weekly, monthly, or annual schedule? What various age-level ministries are offered? Training opportunities? Fill up the circle below by jotting down as many regular or special activities as you can think of. Several typical examples are provided to serve as a catalyst for your thinking. Your church may or may not implement all these examples. (Remember . . . the circle represents the total mix of activities officially planned or sponsored by your church.)

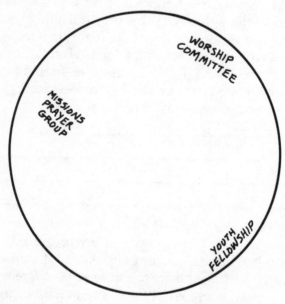

Whew . . . there's more going on than some folks think! A chock-full calendar, though, doesn't automatically make a church effective. Your leaders have the awesome responsibility of planning and evaluating the church's varied ministries on the basis of God-given goals for local churches. Without a sense of direction, or a consciousness of broad purposes at which to aim, they can't be good stewards of the time, energy, and human resources invested in programs.

Most likely, riveted firmly in their minds are guidelines by which to evaluate the health and balance of agencies and programs. They keep in mind questions such as: What are God's goals for this congregation? What should be happening in the lives of Christians as a result of their participation in our ministries? Then, on the basis of Biblically specified functions of the church, they plan and implement particular forms of ministry.

One chunk of Scripture that provides an overarching framework for their planning is Acts 2:41-47. This passage exposes us to the corporate experiences of the first organized group of believers in Jerusalem. From this record of early church life, we can glean some of God's timeless purposes for every local congregation. The scene is Jerusalem on the day of Pentecost. Peter gave a rousing sermon in which he described Jesus as the long-awaited Messiah, described His death and resurrection, and called for repentance. Approximately 3,000 persons accepted Jesus Christ and yielded to baptism.

Read Acts 2:41-47 carefully. Then jot down answers to the following questions.

1. Write a statement describing this band of believers in Jerusalem.

_____

_____

_____

2. What different areas of life or existence were affected by participation in the activities of this church?

_____

_____

_____

3. In the Book of Acts, God provides portraits of early church life in order to communicate enduring principles. This snapshot of the burgeoning church in Jerusalem reveals timeless functions or purposes that every local church in every culture should fulfill. Right now, analyze Acts 2:41-47 and pick out characteristics of a mature church that transcend first-century culture. To put it another way, what goals for all local churches can you glean from the particular experiences of the early church? Pay close attention to specific words and phrases. (Example: verse 42 reads, "They devoted themselves to the apostles' teaching." What timeless function of a church's ministry is couched in that statement?)

_____

_____

_____

_____

Where Do I Fit In?

Look back at the circle in which you wrote various programs and activities sponsored by your church. What justifies the existence of each of those ministries in light of the timeless functions required of a local church? How does each contribute to these functions? Each item on the calendar should exist in order to help accomplish one or more of the timeless purposes of church life, as revealed in your answers to question #3 above.

You may be—or may become—a lay leader in your church. That's why it's important to understand God's goals for all congregations. The timeless goals for church life in Acts 2:41-47 provide a framework for program planning and evaluation. Spiritual growth requires progress in *each* area, not just one or two areas.

These Acts 2 goals can also serve as a frame of reference for individual evaluation. For instance, your list of answers to question #3 probably included "instruction" (teaching) and "authentic fellowship with other Christians." Whereas your leaders have the task of providing opportunities for involvement in these areas, it's your responsibility to tap into those opportunities. Just as a total church calendar must provide a balance of ministries to make sure all of the timeless goals can be reached, so every member of the church should strive for personal spiritual growth in all the areas mentioned.

Lopsided spiritual development occurs if we participate in three instruction-oriented meetings a week, yet seldom take advantage of opportunities to deepen personal relationships with others in the church. Or, it's possible to participate in fellowship-oriented activities to the point of exclusiveness. We may fail to build bridges or relationships with non-Christians, or fail to take advantage of lay witness training provided by the church. As long as we live, God wants us to grow in each of the goals, or "vital experiences," found in Acts 2:41-47.

1. Right now, consider your answers to question #3 in the previous section. Think of specific opportunities your church provides or encourages for development in each area.

a. Over the past year, which of these broad goals for the church have you most noticeably experienced, or been most heavily involved in? (Example: If you've increased your commitment to Bible study groups within the past year, and increased the regularity of your devotional study of God's Word, you might put "instruction.")

_____

_____

b. Which goal of church life has been most lacking in your personal experience over the past year?

_____

c. What can you reasonably do to grow more in this undeveloped area? What developmental opportunities does your church offer in this area? Which one is it feasible to invest in during the coming year?

_____

_____

_____

_____

_____

2. As you ponder your response to the last question, it's important to keep a realistic perspective. Why shouldn't you feel guilty if you can't participate in every program or activity offered by your church or other ministry organizations in your area?

_____

_____

Job commitments and family responsibilities do enter into the picture. God's expectations for your schedule will always be fair. It's true that some churches stuff the calendar with an excessive number of programs, then goad members to invest in almost every one. We aren't encouraging that kind of frantic life-style. Chances are, neither are your church's leaders. We're emphasizing that every Christian needs to make ongoing progress in each timeless goal uncovered in Acts 2. Most opportunities for such growth occur through involvement in activities planned, or supported, by your local church. Persons who yearn for spiritual maturity and ministry effectiveness constantly evaluate their schedule and commitments. They must seek God's wisdom in choosing involvements that result in a balanced, rather than a narrow development.

This week, study the list of the various ministries, and use it as a catalyst for prayer. In your next group meeting, be prepared to share one new idea for ministry that you might feel comfortable implementing in the months ahead.

3

GOD'S PLAN
FOR CHURCH LEADERS

The pastor of a large midwestern church designed a questionnaire listing 14 separate categories of traditional pastoral activity and responsibility (studying, counseling, visitation, committee meetings, teaching, etc.). He gave the questionnaire to 28 lay officers in the church—members of boards and key committees. Each layperson was asked to indicate how many hours per week he or she thought the pastor should devote to each of the 14 categories of responsibility. (Keep in mind that there are 168 total hours in a week. Also, the categories of pastoral activity did not include time for meals, for sleeping, or leisure of any kind.)

By adding the number of hours in each of the 14 categories, you come up with the total number of hours they expected the pastor to work each week. Here are the eye-popping results:

- 18 of the 28 questionnaires totaled more than 100 weekly hours of expected pastoral endeavor.
- 11 of the 28 respondents called for more than 140 hours per week.
- 8 of the 28—no kidding, folks!—expected involvement that totaled more than 168 hours per week!
- Overall, the average weekly expectation was 136.5 hours of pastoral activity per week.

Maybe that's not a typical example. Yet the questionnaires do suggest that many people in church congregations have unrealistic—and unbiblical—expectations of their full-time pastors. In this lesson, let's strip away cultural and historical expectations, and zero in on what God expects of pastors and their associates. Understanding why leadership positions exist is essential. Without this Biblical vantage point, we won't make ongoing ministry involvement a top-shelf priority.

Church Leadership: An Introductory Perspective

In a nutshell, a leader is one who wields influence. By virtue of character, training, and position, such a person has the capacity to produce an effect on other people. You find leaders in all spheres of life: government, business, civic organizations, churches. Within the church, there are numerous positions and responsibilities that can legitimately claim "leadership" status: classroom teachers, chairpersons of committees, program directors, Sunday school superintendents, youth sponsors, board members, and others. To facilitate organization and planning, some positions have more authority than others.

Clearly, the New Testament teaches that Jesus Christ is head of the Church (Col. 1:18). Put simply, the Church is Jesus Christ's physical representative in the realm of time and space. Jesus' headship, though, doesn't negate the need for human leadership in the local church. In fact, God has prescribed that a team of mature individuals manage and guide the spiritual and organizational life of the church. The leadership team consists of the pastoral office—usually occupied by a formally trained person who earns a living in service to the church—and other mature leaders who earn their living in a variety of ways outside the formal work of the church. Passages such as I Timothy 3 and Titus 1 provide a more detailed look at the qualifications and duties of these leaders (usually called "elders" and/or "deacons") in local churches.

Though certain offices and leadership responsibilities are apparently prescribed by Scripture, there is room for flexibility as to how local churches and denominational bodies carry out the business of the church. Many scholars feel the New Testament allows for some diversity in forms of church government—a variety reflected in procedural and decision-making differences at both the denominational and local church levels.

It is not within the scope of this lesson to argue for one form of church government over another. In fact, getting bogged down in such a discussion would make it easy to gloss over the more basic question: What is God's job description for key leaders in the church? Broadly speaking, why do vocational staff positions exist? Whether your church is denominationally aligned or independent, the answer to those questions is the same. (Though the answer has applications to persons at all levels of church leadership, we'll apply it more specifically to the pastoral staff, or vocational leaders.)

To review, stated very simply, a leader is a person who: _____ .

The head of the church is _____, but His rule doesn't negate the need for _____ leadership.

No matter what form of church government a local congregation has, the overarching responsibility of the vocational staff is the same.

Divine Job Description

1. Open your Bible to Ephesians 4:7-16. Read the verses carefully, and summarize the basic theme:

_____

_____

_____

Paul distinguishes between "gifts"—God-given capacities for service which help a church reach its potential—and leadership offices. Every believer has at least one spiritual gift (vs. 7), but not every believer has been appointed for an official position of leadership (some of which are mentioned in vs. 11). Here, Paul clearly points out that believers cannot reach maturity, and the church can't reflect beauty, unless persons in official leadership roles carry out their God-intended functions.

2. Now zero in on verses 11 and 12.

a. Jot down the word or phrase from verse 12 that most precisely describes the church leader's purpose for being:

_____

b. Next, find the one word that tells who is primarily responsible for "works of service," which build up the body of Christ:

_____

c. Now go back to the opening anecdote in this lesson about the 28 officers who completed a questionnaire regarding pastoral responsibilities. Based on Ephesians 4:11, 12, write a paragraph evaluating their expectations of their pastor. (To put it another way, if you could sit down and talk to these 28 laypersons, what would you tell them?)

_____

_____

_____

_____

_____

In the next meeting of your LAMP group, your leader will further clarify the apostle Paul's teaching concerning the church, found in Ephesians 4:11, 12. Right now, though, mull over the following quotes by well-known authors about the role of church leaders. As you digest these statements, evaluate your written responses to the previous study exercises.

The local church essentially is a training place to equip Christians to carry out their own ministries. Unfortunately, for many Christians the church is a place to go to watch professionals perform and to pay the professionals to carry out the church program. In many quarters Christianity has deteriorated into professional "pulpitism" financed by lay spectators. The church hires a staff of ministers to do all the Christian service. This scheme is not only a violation of God's plan, but an absolute detriment to the growth of the church and the vitality of the members of the Body. Every member needs to find a significant place of service. To limit the work of the ministry to a small, select class of full-time clergymen hinders the spiritual growth of God's people, stunts the discipleship process in the Body, and the evangelistic outreach of the church into the community.
—John MacArthur, Jr., *Body Dynamics* (Victor Books)

The declaration of Ephesians 4 is that the ultimate work of the church in the world is to be done by the saints—plain, ordinary Christians—and not by a professional clergy or a few select laymen. The four offices of apostle, prophet, evangelist, and pastor-teacher exist for but one function: that of equipping the common Christians to do the tasks which are assigned to them. Perhaps this can be made clearer if we diagram verses 11 and 12 in the following manner:

Apostles	***Do one thing:***	***Unto:*** *the work of the*
Prophets	*Equip the*	*ministry, unto, the*
Evangelists	*saints*	*upbuilding of the*
Pastor-teachers		*Body of Christ*

—Ray Stedman, *Body Life* (Regal Books)

31

In addition to whatever else it may be, the gift of pastoring is a catalyst geared to release the gift potential of those in the flock.
—Kenneth O. Gangel, *Unwrap Your Spiritual Gifts* (Victor Books)

The pastor's major job is to help others minister—not do all the work of ministry himself.
—Joe Aldrich, *Lifestyle Evangelism* (Multnomah Press)

How ridiculous it would be if football coaches yanked their starting lineup off the field, and inserted themselves into the game to run the plays. Yet, too often, that's what church leaders are doing! The leaders are the "star players" who pass, block, and kick—while spectators watch and clap. But our job as leaders is to coach the church members so they can get into the game and succeed—while we clap and offer support from the sidelines. Like coaches, church leaders are successful when they've prepared others to get the job done.
—Bruce Wilkinson (President of Walk Thru the Bible Ministries)

Many times the clergy, not understanding clearly their role, have let their ministry be determined by the places where the pressures were the greatest. As a result, they have been very unhappy and have found no fulfillment in the ministry. On the other hand, the laity, through lack of understanding, have placed responsibilities upon the clergy which tended to exploit them and did not permit the fulfillment of their call. It would be a tremendously releasing experience both for the clergy and the laity if both came to understand the nature of the specific "calling" of the clergy, as seen in Ephesians 4:11, 12.

God has called the laity to be His basic ministers. He has called some to be "player-coaches" (to use Elton Trueblood's term) to equip the laity for the ministry they are to fulfill. This is a radical departure from the traditional understanding of the roles of the laity and the clergy. The laity had the idea that they were already committed to a "full-time" vocation in the secular world, thus they did not have time—at least much time—to do God's work. Therefore they contributed money to "free" the clergy to have the time needed to fulfill God's ministry. This view is rank heresy.
—Findley B. Edge, *The Greening of the Church* (Word Books)

Before moving to the final phase of the lesson . . .

3. Put an asterisk beside the quotation that you consider most to the point or illuminating.

4. Underline *one sentence* from one of the quotes which, in your opinion, best clarifies the theme of this lesson.

An Elevated Role

In the next group session, you'll learn more about the "equipping" role of local church leaders. You'll also discover specific ways the leaders in your church try to fulfill the mandate of Ephesians 4:12. Right now, though, it's imperative to realize that coaching and preparing others to serve elevates, rather than reduces, the significance of leadership roles. Strong, and sometimes authoritative, leadership must still be exerted in the church by members of the pastoral staff and governing board.

For instance, emphasizing the "coach" rather than "star player" analogy should not create a namby-pamby or laissez-faire attitude toward church leaders. While it is true that members of a congregation deserve the title "minister" just as much as the vocational pastor, that truth doesn't give them the license to undermine the pastor's leadership. Their attitude of "followship" remains a key ingredient of a healthy church.

1. Look up I Timothy 5:17-19, and Hebrews 13:7, 17, 18.

a. What attitudes toward church leaders are called for in these verses?

_____

_____

_____

b. Specifically, what actions in response to leaders does the Lord encourage?

_____

_____

_____

2. How do these Biblical concepts confirm or change
your previous thinking about church leadership?

_____

_____

_____

_____

Support Your Local Pastor!

One of the responses called for in Hebrews 13:18 is
prayer. Leadership can be a tough, gut-wrenching role.
And the higher the position, the greater the accountability and pressure. You can honor your pastor and
other members of the leadership team by praying on a
regular basis for them.

Can you sign the following pledge?

I promise before God to pray for _____
at least once each week for the duration of this *Welcome
to Your Ministry* course.

Signed _____

If you signed it, why not drop that person a note in
the mail and inform him or her of your prayer commitment. Also ask if there are specific requests that you
can pray about on their behalf. So often leaders hear
from members of the congregation only when they
have a complaint. Dare to be different—and you'll
make their jobs a little easier!

4

YOU HAVE THE CALL OF A MINISTER

On the lawn of most church facilities, you see a large sign that contains information for the public. A typical sign reads:

CHURCH OF THE REDEEMER
MINISTER: REV. JOHN SMITH

In Lessons 1-3, you learned a few basic concepts about ministry, the church, and church leadership. Based on what you've gleaned from these lessons, how would you change the wording of the above sign? What could you print on the sign that would more accurately capture the truths you've covered?

(Design your own sign below. In as few words as possible, it should reflect two or more basic conclusions we've made so far.)

A Historical Perspective

So far, you've learned that every believer—regardless of vocation and background—is to accomplish God's work in the world. The primary agency that God uses to accomplish His work is the local church. Through a give-and-take relationship with a church, the individual believer is nurtured to a point of usefulness in the world. Church leaders exist, not to do all the work of ministry, but to equip members of the congregation for their varied service roles.

Now that we've surveyed how the local church relates to the theme of ministry, let's zero in on the basic assumption of the course once again. We've introduced the idea that *every Christian is a minister*. Let's look closer at the Biblical roots of this idea.

Because it is firmly rooted in the New Testament, the concept of "every Christian a minister" isn't new. However, it hasn't penetrated the thinking of believers throughout church history.

Historically, Christians have driven a wedge between the roles of the "clergy" and the "laity." We've employed those terms in a way that depicts the clergy as a select group of professionals who are called and formally educated to do the work of the church, and the laity as a responsive audience. This distinction, though, is not Biblical.

The New Testament word for laity is *laos*. Simply translated, it means "people." It is used scores of times in the New Testament.

1. Look up the following references, and jot down any observations you can make about how the term *laos* is used. (When you have more than one verse to read, the verse in which the term is found is in italics.)

a. Matthew 1:20, *21* _____

_____

b. II Corinthians 6:*16*-18 _____

_____

c. Titus 2:11-*14* _____

_____

d. I Peter 2:*9*, *10* (See I Pet. 1:1, 2 for a glimpse at Peter's reading audience.)

_____

_____

2. The term has a limited scope. It refers to believers in general, but not specifically to persons who serve in leadership capacities. (True or false?) ____

3. The word clergy (*kleros* in Greek) is also found in the New Testament. Literally, the term means "lot, share, portion, or inheritance." How is it used in the following references? (Pick out the English word that you believe is the translation for *kleros*. Briefly summarize what it means in the context.)

a. Colossians 1:12; Acts 20:32

_____

_____

b. Acts 1:17 (See verses 12-26 for context.)

_____

_____

c. I Peter 5:1-3. Each elder whom Peter addresses may have had spiritual responsibility for a portion of a given congregation. A form of the word clergy is employed in verse 3. It refers to people "allotted" to the care of an elder. With that backdrop, comment on how the word is used in verse 3, compared to how we employ the term today.

_____

_____

d. To sum up, put true or false after the following statement: When designating a group of people, the term that we translate "clergy" encompasses *all* believers who have a share in the benefits (inheritance) of salvation. It refers to Christians who *aren't* leaders as well as those who are. ____

37

In your next group session, your leader will crystallize the difference between the Bible's use of these terms, and our traditional use of them. You'll discover how the words evolved after the first century. You'll also understand more vividly how our terminology is either a help or hindrance to a life-style of service.

A Biblical Perspective

The way we normally use the terms "clergy" and "laity" suggests that only a few are "called" into Christian ministry. You've discovered, however, that *all* Christians are God's laity, and *all* Christians are God's clergy! Only a few are called to earn their living in a ministry position (see Lesson 3), but all believers are called into God's service. In *The Greening of the Church*, Findley Edge puts it this way:

The call to salvation and the call to the ministry is one and the same call. That is, when one is called by God to be a part of His people, he is also called into the ministry. Young people often struggle with the question as to whether or not they are "called into the ministry." From one perspective, this is a completely irrelevant question. If a person has been called by God to be a Christian, then he has been called into the ministry.

Edge's assertion doesn't deny that there's a special and separate calling for vocational Christian work. Nor does he deny that there's a lofty, specialized role for vocational leaders to play—as described in Lesson 3. He's simply making the point that *service isn't optional for nonvocational workers.*

Numerous New Testament passages affirm this call of every believer into ministry. In Lesson 1 you saw that service is one of God's ultimate objectives for every believer. You examined several passages and selected key phrases that revealed this objective (Jn. 15:5, 8, 16; II Cor. 5:17-20; and I Pet. 2:9, 10). Turn back in your book and review those phrases again (see pages 14 and

15). Also, in Lesson 3 you dissected Ephesians 4:12. That verse calls for "saints"—all members of the congregation, not just persons in leadership offices—to perform "works of service."

Look up these additional verses, which reinforce the same truth. From them, describe in your own words what the Bible teaches about every Christian being called to help accomplish God's work in the world.

Ephesians 2:8-10 _____

_____

Matthew 5:13-16 _____

_____

I Peter 4:10, 11 _____

_____

Now go back and put Matthew 5:16 and I Peter 4:11 under your mental microscope. What words from these verses reveal the ultimate result, or consequence, of obeying God's call to a life-style of ministry?

_____

_____

_____

Fulfilling Your Call

During the past week, in what concrete ways have you fulfilled this divine calling? What are some ways the Lord has used you? (Remember: ministry may be exercised in a public or formal position in the gathered church setting, or it may be an informal, behind-the-scenes endeavor. A phone conversation, a letter, a lunch appointment, a coaching opportunity, a hospital visit—you name it!—can become a sacred context for serving the purposes of God in the world.)

_____

_____

_____

_____

_____

Whether or not you can identify the spiritual results of these acts of service, pray right now for the Lord to honor Himself through them. Ask the Lord to fertilize and water the seeds you sowed in word or deed.

Now shift your attention to the coming week. Think of meetings, appointments, mundane duties, social gatherings—anything on tap! Within the sphere of these nitty-gritty roles and relationships, how is the Lord calling you to minister to others in His name? Jot down a few possibilities here.

_____

_____

_____

_____

_____

_____

_____

As you look for opportunities to fulfill your ministry, keep in mind what author Elton Trueblood tells believers who are not in vocational ministry:

When I talk with people, I don't call them laymen. A layman is a second-class citizen. I am a layman in regard to law because I haven't passed the bar exam; thus, I am not allowed to practice law. There is no place in the church of Jesus Christ for those who cannot practice. I say to people, "You are not a layman. You are a minister of common life."
—Leadership Journal (Winter, 1983)

5

YOU HAVE THE TITLE OF A MINISTER

The Scripture declares, "according as each hath received a gift, ministering it among yourselves, as good stewards of the manifold grace of God . . ." (I Pet. 4:10). From this passage it can be seen that every Christian has a ministry for which he is accountable to God. On this point there is no difference between clergy and laity. Thus when the layman is confronted with the opportunity to serve in the church, the question for him is not whether he has a ministry, but whether this particular form of ministry is the one to which God is calling him and for which He will hold him accountable.

This attitude runs directly counter to the practice of voluntarism, a habit deeply ingrained in American church life and devastating in its effects. By voluntarism I mean the notion that ministry is optional for the layman. If a layman rejected an opportunity for service in the church, all concerned react with indifference, or, at most, disappointment. On the other hand, if he accepts an invitation for ministry, he is looked upon as having granted the church a favor.

—Norman E. Harper, *Making Disciples*

A Biblical Mandate

In the New Testament, the Church is depicted as a Kingdom—not a volunteer agency! That statement stems from concepts already explored in this course. What are some implications of this statement for someone who joins a local church?

Joining a church and remaining passive isn't a valid option. Our King, Jesus Christ, has issued decrees making the work of the church the responsibility of every member. (See the Scriptures in Lesson 4.) Each lesson in this course tries to refute the view that ministry involvement is merely a "volunteer" endeavor, rather than a Biblical mandate.

In this week's lesson, you'll do more spadework on the concept of ministry. You'll discover that the Biblical roots of the "every Christian a minister" theme go deeper and stretch farther than you ever imagined! Last week you learned that a call to ministry is included in the call to salvation. In this lesson, you'll discover that God has given you *titles* to go with the call.

The Title of 'Minister'

The most common word for "minister" in the original Greek of the New Testament, *diakonos*, means "servant," "attendant," or "deacon." The verb form means "to wait upon" or "to serve." Though it is the term used to describe the office of "deacon" in I Timothy, most usages have no relationship to that official leadership capacity in the church.

The following references use some form of the Greek word *diakonos*. Examine each reference carefully, find the English translation of the word, and in your own words describe how this term is used. (Pay special attention to personalities, to the intended recipients of commands, deeds mentioned, etc. When more than one verse is listed, the verses in which the term occurs are in italics.)

Mark 1:30, *31* _____

_____

John 12:26 _____

_____

Matthew 20:25-28 _____

_____

Matthew 25:44 (read vss. 31-46 for context) _____

_____

Romans 16:1, 2 _____

_____

II Corinthians 5:18 (vss. 17-20 for context) _____

_____

II Corinthians 8:4; 9:1 _____

_____

Colossians 1:23, 25 _____

_____

II Timothy 1:16-18 _____

_____

I Peter 4:10, 11 _____

_____

Hebrews 6:9, 10 _____

_____

Now think analytically for a few moments. Mull over
the gleanings from the word study. Jot down any conclusions or observations that you deem important:

_____

_____

_____

_____

_____

_____

_____

Based on your Scripture search, why is it inappropriate to reserve the title "minister" only for persons in vocational church leadership?

_____

_____

The Title of 'Priest'

The designation "priest" may conjure up (for some people) images of formal, ritualistic religion: the Old Testament sacrificial system, for example, with its ornate Temple and elaborate vestments. For Protestants, in particular, it may seem strange to apply the term to describe all members of Christ's Church. But the Scripture does!

Crack open your Bible to I Peter 2:4-10 and Revelation 1:3-6. Read these passages slowly. Peter calls the Church a "holy priesthood" (I Pet. 2:5), and a "royal priesthood" (I Pet. 2:9). John asserts that through Jesus' death, we've been made "a kingdom and priests to serve his God and Father" (Rev. 1:6).

Put simply, in the Old Testament era the priesthood was an office. God prescribed that certain people serve as priests. One of the main functions of a priest was to serve as a mediator between the people and God. The priest literally offered up sacrifices to God on their behalf. The Book of Leviticus describes in elaborate detail the various sacrifices God required, and the related priestly duties. The holiness of God and the sinfulness of the people made these sacrifices necessary, with their ultimate purpose being reconciliation with God.

Shifting to the New Testament, we observe that the Book of Hebrews portrays Jesus Christ as the great High Priest. He was the ultimate and final mediator

44

between humanity and God. His death on the cross was the once-and-for-all sacrifice that made possible reconciliation between sinful people and a Holy God. His sacrifice made the Jewish sacrificial system obsolete. No longer do we have to go through an imperfect human mediator in order to reach God. Thanks to the cross, we now have the privilege of direct access to God. (For background, read Hebrews 7-10.)

In the Old Testament era, priests offered some foreign object as a sacrifice (a lamb, dove, grain, etc.). But Jesus' High Priesthood was different in that He didn't offer up some foreign object on behalf of a sinful world. He offered Himself. His own life was the sacrifice!

With that background material serving as food for thought, perhaps we can better understand I Peter 2:5. Here Peter called the Church a holy priesthood and said that we are expected to offer up "spiritual sacrifices acceptable to God." In light of Jesus' example as a priest, what did Peter mean? In your own words, describe the "spiritual sacrifices" we are expected to offer up today.

_____

_____

_____

_____

_____

Also read Romans 12:1. What light does this verse shed on the meaning of I Peter 2:5? How does this verse help clarify the mandate to "offer up spiritual sacrifices"?

_____

_____

_____

_____

In the next group session, your group leader will explain and further clarify the meaning and relevance of I Peter 2:5 for believers today. For now, just allow the main points from this lesson to become firmly entrenched in your mind. If you're a Christian, the New Testament bestows upon you two significant titles: you are a minister, as well as a priest!

To Keep It, Give It Away!

Research among educational experts shows that we retain more information for a longer period of time if we either verbalize it to another person, or communicate it in writing. Why not increase your retention of key truths from Lessons 1-5 by sharing what you've learned in either a telephone conversation, or letter. What you share may benefit the other person as well!

A few weeks ago, you were asked to write a thank-you note to a "lay" Christian whom the Lord has used in your life. You were also instructed to solicit that person's prayers as you progress through this course. That person would be an ideal recipient of this phone call or letter! Make the contact a kind of "progress report" of concepts you're learning, and differences the Lord is making in your life.

Whether the context is the phone, a letter, a living room conversation, or a formal teaching opportunity, get in the habit of sharing what you're learning. God never teaches us or blesses us solely for our own benefit.

Another alternative is to ask God to bring one Christian into your life with whom you could meet on a weekly basis. You could obtain a *Welcome to Your Minis-*

try study guide for this person, and go over each lesson together when you meet. Because this informal discipling context wouldn't require you to serve as a teacher in a formal sense, the opportunity shouldn't be too threatening. If you pursue such a ministry, though, you'll want to obtain a **Leader's Guide** for the course from your church. Also, before you ask someone to join you in such a one-on-one adventure, be sure to spell out the costs. An hour or so of homework will be necessary for him or her, just as it is for you.

Please don't take this discipling suggestion lightly. In some form or another, God wants you to use your completed workbook as a means of conveying His Word to others. When you've finished this course, one measure of its impact on your life will be whether or not it gathers dust on a bookshelf.

6

YOU HAVE THE RESOURCES OF A MINISTER

God always equips us for what He calls us to do.

When you think of your involvement in God's work in the world, how does the above maxim make you feel? Jot down two or three "feeling words" here:

In the two previous lessons, you've inspected Bible passages that give every believer both the title of "minister," and the divine call to be involved in ministry. This lesson shows that God's ministry mandate is quite realistic. God provides the supernatural resources necessary to fulfill the various ministries He assigns us. Generally speaking, His resources include the Holy Spirit, the written Word, and prayer. But the specific slant of this lesson is spiritual giftedness. What the Bible calls "spiritual gifts" proves that God doesn't merely command us to serve, then leave us dangling without assistance.

What ARE Spiritual Gifts?

The original Greek word for "gift," *charisma*, means "a capacity or ability that is graciously and freely given." It is a form of the Greek word for "grace." The use of this term points to our unworthiness for such gifts. There is nothing in us that deserves such a resource. The initiative lies entirely with the Lord. The word "spiritual" simply refers to the fact that any capacity for service is "caused by the divine Spirit." A gift is nothing we can boast about, since it never originates with us.

Summarize the previous paragraph *in your own words*. Write a one-sentence definition of spiritual gifts.

_____

_____

What Basic Truths About Gifts Should I Know?

Read Romans 12:3-8; I Corinthians 12:4-27; Ephesians 4:7-16; and I Peter 4:10, 11. Don't merely skim these passages. Go over each one slowly, and digest the material. Then answer the following questions.

1. Who receives spiritual gifts? Find phrases from the Bible passages above that reveal the scope of God's enablement for ministry.

_____

_____

_____

2. What is the relationship between spiritual giftedness and the analogy of the Church as the Body of Christ?

_____

_____

_____

3. What phrases from these texts point to the overarching purposes, or consequences, of spiritual gifts being exercised by believers? (Pay special attention to I Cor. 12:7; Eph. 4:12-16; and I Pet. 4:11.)

_____

_____

_____

_____

_____

4. What specific gifts, or capacities for service, can you find in these passages? Do a comparative study and compile a "master list" of gifts mentioned in these passages. (Be aware that some gifts will be mentioned more than once.)

_____   _____

_____   _____

_____   _____

_____   _____

_____   _____

5. Study your master list of gifts for a moment. What general observations about giftedness and ministry can you make?

_____

_____

_____

_____

6. Now put together what you've learned and jot down responses to this question: What negative personal attitudes, commonly experienced by Christians, should be eliminated by the teaching on spiritual gifts?

_____

_____

_____

_____

How Am I Gifted?

If you can't identify your spiritual gifts with any degree of certainty, don't feel all shot down! A lot of other Christians are in the same boat. In the next group meeting, your leader will spend several minutes on the theme of "how to discover your spiritual gifts." So if you have no inkling at all, skip over this section of the workbook. Spend several minutes in prayer, asking God to begin revealing how He has equipped you for serving Him. However, if you think you have a particular gift—even if you aren't sure—try to answer the following questions.

1. What gift (or gifts) do you feel God has given you?

---

2. What is the basis for your answer to the previous question? That is, how has the Lord confirmed those capacities for service in your life?

---

3. In what specific settings, or contexts, have you exercised the gift(s) listed previously?

---

4. Brainstorm for a minute. What are some possible ways your area(s) of giftedness could be used by the Lord in the future? (Think of both formal and informal contexts—that is, roles within the church program, as well as opportunities outside of formal positions in the

church. Don't confine yourself to traditional roles and categories. Be imaginative.)

_____

_____

_____

_____

_____

Questions

You're probably aware that believers disagree over certain facets of the subject of spiritual gifts. Obviously, one lesson on the subject cannot resolve these issues. In fact, we've tried to focus on fundamental points of agreement rather than particular areas of controversy. If your church has distinctive beliefs regarding aspects of this subject, your leader may choose to explain these during the next group meeting.

Since the scope of this lesson is necessarily limited, it may have raised some questions, as well as provided some answers. Right now, jot down questions on the theme of spiritual gifts that you would most like your group leader or pastor to answer. Limit your questions to three, and write them in order of priority. (Not all these questions will be resolved in the next group session. But your leader can channel them to your pastor, who might wish to visit your class, or use the questions as food for thought while preparing a future sermon on this subject.)

_____

_____

_____

_____

_____

In the Meantime

At least two areas of application stem from this study. First, you may wish to delve deeper into this subject by reading one of the following books. (This bibliography is far from exhaustive. Consider asking your study group leader or pastor for the book on spiritual gifts that he or she most heartily recommends.) Through your own initiative and research, you can find answers to many of your questions, and clarify more specifically how God has put you together to serve Him in this world.

Spiritual Gift Resources:

Clinton, Bobby. *Spiritual Gifts* (Learning Resource Center, World Team and Co.)

Flynn, Leslie. *19 Gifts of the Spirit* (Victor Books)

Stedman, Ray. *Body Life* (Regal)

Wagner, Peter. *Spiritual Gifts Can Help Your Church Grow* (Regal)

Second, think of one Christian who has exercised a particular gift in the past (teaching, administration, giving, etc.), but who seems less active for the Lord in recent years or months. This may be a person in your current church, or someone you knew years ago in another city. Drop that person a note and inform him or her of the gift you recognized, and of the edification that resulted from good stewardship of it. Encourage him or her to continue using that capacity for service, and not to let it become dormant. Be sure, though, to keep the tone of your note positive. There may be factors you aren't aware of that have caused the person to become less involved in ministry. Your purpose isn't to condemn, but to affirm and to stimulate.

Or, consider this alternative application. Think of a member of your current LAMP study group who has a particular capacity for service. Perhaps you sense that one participant, based on his zeal and ability to express himself, would make a good teacher. Perhaps another has an unusual knack for encouraging others. Or when you divide into smaller groups, perhaps you've noticed that one person in particular keeps the group organized and the discussion on track. Pen a note to this person before the next group meeting. Point out the ministry capacity that you've observed—whether or not you can technically label it a "spiritual gift"—and thank the individual for what he or she has contributed to the group meetings.

7

HOW TO MARK A LIFE FOR CHRIST

The *Christian Herald* once carried an article about a senior executive of one of the largest banks in New York City. He told how he had risen to a place of prominence and influence. At first he served as an office boy. Then one day the president of the company called him aside and said, "I want you to come into my office and be with me each day." The young man replied, "But what could I do to help you, sir? I don't know anything about finances."

"Never mind that! You will learn what I want to teach you a lot faster if you *just stay by my side* and keep your eyes and ears open!"

"That was the most significant experience of my life," said the now-famous banker. "Being with that wise man made me just like him. I began to do things the way he did, and that accounts for what I am today."

Caring Counts

Whether in business or in the Christian life, individuals with experience can have great influence upon those who are just beginning. But they must care enough to give their time and energy. Think of an individual from your past who contributed to your spiritual development. This person may have ministered to you through a position in a church program

(Sunday school teacher, youth sponsor, etc.) or may have contributed to your life through a role outside of an official church position (schoolteacher, parent, close friend, etc.). Jot down his or her name:

_____

Now write a concise response to these questions: What do I remember most about this person? How did this individual mark my life for Jesus Christ?

_____

_____

_____

_____

_____

_____

Next, mull over what you just wrote about this person. What conclusions and/or observations can you make about ministry, or Christian leadership, by analyzing this person's impact on your life?

_____

_____

_____

_____

_____

Because they're rooted in your personal experience, any genuine answers to the previous questions are valid. Most of us, though, when recalling persons who have marked our lives for Christ, think of character qualities or practical expressions of concern. Even when the person we think of served in a skilled capacity such as teaching, what we remember most is rarely his or her Bible knowledge, polished methodology, oratorical ability, or magnetic personality. What we remember most about people who change our lives is their love for us. Responses like the following are common:

- My junior high teacher made me feel special because he always greeted me by name when I entered the classroom, and asked questions about how my week had gone.
- She consistently wrote letters of encouragement during my first year away at college.
- She helped me stay close to the Lord by praying for me, and sending me a gift subscription to a Christian magazine for teens.
- He'd listen to me. I felt he really wanted to know about my feelings and problems.

No matter what our spiritual gifts are, or what leadership positions we accept in the church, the key to influencing a life for Christ is *genuine concern* for that person. Things like Bible knowledge and skills training are important, but warm relationships, filled with genuine caring, must undergird all ministry endeavors.

Lessons 1-6 of this course examined the Biblical basis for the everyone-is-a-minister theme. Through a variety of Bible passages, the mandate for ministry should have been stamped indelibly on our minds. Beginning with Lesson 7, the focus will shift a bit. We'll get even more practical by probing a few specific ways to influence others spiritually. The avenues of influence we'll cover can be applied to a wide spectrum of ministry positions or service capacities—both within and outside the formal church program. The fundamental thesis in Lesson 7 is this: *Genuine caring enhances the potential of any service that is rendered in the name of Christ.* Let's look at some Biblical examples of this truth, and consider practical ways to express concern in various ministry roles.

A Personal Approach

The apostle Paul is a case in point. Paul founded the church in Philippi. Later, while in prison, he penned a letter to this new congregation. He wrote to thank them for their financial support, and to encourage and instruct them in the faith.

1. Read Philippians 1:1-11 and jot down several words that describe the tone (or relational "atmosphere") of the letter.

_____

_____

_____

2. Read the passage a second time. Locate key words and phrases directly from the text that reveal Paul's personal concern for the people, and a relational style of leadership.

_____

_____

_____

3. Now turn to I Thessalonians 2:7-11. Here Paul is reminiscing about his former ministry among the Thessalonians. From these five verses, what words and/or phrases reveal Paul's deep, personal concern for the people?

_____

_____

_____

Scripture teems with examples of teachers, evangelists, and administrators who viewed ministry as an investment in people. They not only spoke God's words and administered religious tasks, but they genuinely cared for the persons they served. Their leadership took on a personal, or relational, dimension. Jesus' strategy was also to fuse public ministries such as verbal instruction with authentic interest in each individual He met. Between discourses and miracles, He let frolicsome children relax on His lap. Once, when a swarm of people encircled Him, He treated the particular needs of a synagogue official whose daughter was dying, and of a woman whose illness had vexed her for twelve years. Also, He balanced ministry to multitudes with an in-depth investment of time in twelve individual disciples. "He appointed twelve . . . that they might be with him" (Mk. 3:14). As Robert Coleman put it in *The Master Plan of Evangelism*, "knowledge was gained by association before it was understood by explanation."

Today, as it was in Bible times, we need to equate "ministry" with nitty-gritty investments in people. Such investments necessarily involve spending significant chunks of time with them. When we sacrifice our time for others, they perceive us as "caring," and we're apt to influence their lives for Christ.

How Caring Shows

As a rule, people have trouble applying a general concept—even one as down-to-earth as "be a caring person." We're more apt to obey a concept when it is broken down—when we intentionally think of possible ways to apply it in various spheres of life. Concrete examples of a command or concept give us more food for thought.

The four categories below represent four common spheres of ministry: teaching (in a Sunday school, home Bible study, discipleship group); administration (through positions such as Sunday school superintendent, church committee membership, board membership, program chairperson); evangelism (whether attempted through a church outreach program, or informal witnessing efforts in your neighborhood or at work); and service, (often behind-the-scenes acts of assisting or showing mercy). Brainstorm for a few minutes, and jot down several specific ways to express concern in each sphere of ministry.

1. Teaching: In what concrete ways would a "caring, relational" teaching style show up?

_____

_____

_____

_____

2. Administration: How can an administrator who is responsible for getting things done show concern for people with whom and for whom he or she works?

_____

_____

_____

_____

3. Evangelism: What forms might caring take when we're trying to win a person to Christ?

_____

_____

_____

_____

4. Service: What are some examples of nonpublic, behind-the-scenes, need-meeting acts of service?

_____

_____

_____

_____

_____

5. In which one of these four basic realms are you predominantly ministering at this time?

_____

6. In which of these spheres of ministry do you anticipate the most involvement in future years?

_____

7. Now, mull over the "ways to express care" that you listed for this particular ministry role. Personalize the list by jotting down two ways you can be a more caring person in your particular sphere of responsibility and influence.

_____

_____

_____

_____

Ask the Lord to help you incorporate these ideas in the months ahead. After all, showing Christlike love for others is a supernatural endeavor. In our own strength, we're far too self-centered to make caring a life-style. But by regularly tapping into His resources, we can "do immeasurably more than all we ask or imagine, according to his power that is at work within us" (Eph. 3:20).

8

THE MINISTRY OF ENCOURAGEMENT

Let's imagine that our Lord is in the newspaper business. He's publisher of the *Pearly Gate Gazette*. You turn to the want ad section, and a large, boldface ad leaps out at you:

IMMEDIATE OPENINGS!

The Kingdom of God has immediate openings for persons who . . .

- Want to make a lasting impact on others' lives
- Feel inferior or inadequate because they think they have few skills and abilities to offer God
- Feel overshadowed by publicly gifted servants

QUALIFICATIONS: Neither a clerical robe nor seminary degree is needed. The only requirements are a personal relationship with Christ, and a willingness to get involved in the lives of others.

WORKING CONDITIONS: You can carry out this responsibility in the nitty-gritty of your daily schedule—whether you're a business executive, doctor, lawyer, teacher, or diaper changer. It isn't a "Sunday only" ministry that occurs solely within the walls of your church building. It's a life-style. Be aware, though, that it's often an unsung, behind-the-scenes position. It won't bring you public applause, nor earn you headlines in this newspaper. In fact, the price you pay for this ministry is high: your time, abilities, material resources—you name it—must be at the complete disposal of Jesus Christ.

JOB BENEFITS: You'll receive a hearty "well done!" from your Lord— and you'll experience the satisfaction of knowing that you redirected the course of peoples' lives for the better.

APPLY TODAY for the position of "Encourager."

An Essential Ministry

Are you willing to "buy into" the ministry of encouragement? No matter what your spiritual gifts are, and what Christian service positions you hold, you can deepen or supplement current endeavors for God by consciously exercising this taken-for-granted ministry. In Lesson 7, you discovered that one key to "marking" lives for Jesus Christ is caring. Lessons 8-10 are practical extensions of Lesson 7. These lessons suggest concrete ways to care for others—for the ultimate purpose of advancing Christ's Kingdom.

Make no mistake about it, the ministry of encouragement is potential packed. It's a lubricant for human relationships. Let's find out what God says about this essential avenue of service.

What's in a Name?

Perhaps the most meaningful way to approach this subject is to examine the life of someone who modeled encouragement. Scripture abounds with personalities who exercised this ministry, but only one person had a name that actually meant "encouragement." That individual was named Barnabas, which means "Son of Encouragement." Originally, his name was Joseph. But members of the early church in Jerusalem honored him by changing his name to Barnabas. They observed his extraordinary knack of encouraging others, and they wanted his name to reflect his behavior.

Several episodes in the Book of Acts show Barnabas in action. Read the following selections carefully. You can use the same question to analyze each passage: "What did Barnabas do to earn the title of Encourager?" Pay close attention to the individuals or groups whom Barnabas encouraged. Imagine that you're the individual, or part of the group, on the receiving end. Jot down answers to the study questions by pinpointing specific words and/or actions of Barnabas acting as an encourager.

What did Barnabas do to earn the title "Encourager"?
Acts 4:32-37 _____

_____

_____

Acts 9:26-28 (Skim 9:1-25 for necessary background.)

_____

_____

_____

Acts 11:19-26 _____

_____

_____

Acts 15:36-41 (John Mark had deserted Paul and Barnabas during the first missionary journey. This dialogue occurs immediately preceding Paul's second missionary trek.)

_____

_____

_____

A Close-up Portrait

So far you've listed the primary ways Barnabas encouraged others. Now let's take an even closer look at the portrait of this man in Acts. We want to glean timeless principles of encouragement that are just as applicable today as they were in the first century. Review the four episodes again, and answer these questions:

1. Which instance of encouragement impresses you most? Why?

_____

_____

_____

_____

2. Based on what he said and did, plus what is directly stated about him in these episodes, what character qualities did Barnabas have?

_____

_____

_____

_____

3. Of the character qualities you listed in #2, which two personal traits do you think are most vital to an on-going ministry of encouragement? Why?

_____

_____

_____

_____

4. Now you're ready to summarize the timeless nuggets from these narratives:

a. Compile a "master list" of specific ways Barnabas encouraged others.

_____

_____

_____

_____

_____

_____

b. Write several timeless principles of encouragement that you see in these episodes, and jot down evidences for each principle you write. (Example: Encouraging others is sometimes a costly ministry. Barnabas sacrificed his property for the work of the church: Acts 4. He risked his own reputation in standing up for Paul: Acts 9. He gave up a more public ministry with Paul to reassure, and to invest in John Mark: Acts 15.)

_____

_____

_____

_____

_____

_____

c. Before moving to the last phase of this lesson, think through ways that others have encouraged you, or other members of your family, in recent years. What types, or forms, of encouragement can you add to the list in question A above? (What Barnabas did doesn't exhaust the possible avenues encouragement can take!)

_____

_____

_____

_____

_____

_____

_____

Encouragement in Action

Right now, ask the Lord to give you the name of one individual or family who may have a special need for encouragement at this time. (Think of persons who've

experienced illness, financial reverses, relational con-
flicts, peace-robbing job pressures, etc.)

Put the name of the person/family here:

_____

Using the content of your Barnabas study as a catalyst for your thinking, list one or two concrete ways you
can serve as a "Barnabas" to this person or family
during the coming week.

_____

_____

_____

Also, if you're currently involved in an ongoing ministry, jot down a couple of ways you can be more of an
encourager in that particular context.

_____

_____

_____

"Barnabas" is no longer a popular name. But your
name doesn't have to mean "Encourager" for you to be
one!

9

THE MINISTRY OF INTERCESSION

Recently, a group of 20 young adults was asked to brainstorm for a list of so-called evangelical clichés. Then, they individually voted on the most commonly heard cliché. Can you guess the winner? "I'll pray for you" easily got the most votes!

How unfortunate. A cliché is any phrase or expression used so frequently and flippantly that it loses its meaning. We hear them daily. Opportunities go "down the drain." As a result, we "cry over spilled milk." But when a pledge to pray is uttered so casually that recipients don't really expect follow-through, it's unimpeachable evidence that we take the ministry of intercession too lightly.

What are some Christian clichés that are heard often in church circles—expressions that are so casually tossed out that their impact is diminished? Jot down a few here:

_____

_____

_____

On Behalf of Others

Put simply, to intercede means to make a request on behalf of another. In Biblical days, the noun form (intercession) was a technical term for approaching a king. We exercise this ministry whenever we approach our God with petitions on behalf of others. Intercession recognizes that no matter what else we do for others (teaching, encouraging, counseling, etc.), the Holy Spirit must do a direct work in their hearts and minds for our ministry to be ultimately effective. This is because *all* forms of ministry on behalf of others are *supernatural* endeavors requiring more than mere human resources. Thus intercession is a vital ingredient in all other efforts to serve others in Jesus' name.

How can we keep "I'll pray for you" from becoming a flippant cliché in our lives? What does God's Word say about this vital ministry? What qualities go hand in glove with a ministry of intercession? Who were some consistent intercessors in the Bible? What are some practical tips that can help us exercise this specialized form of service? The Bible study that follows, in conjunction with your next group meeting, will tackle these questions.

Portrait of an Intercessor: Nehemiah

During the Babylonian Captivity of the Jews, in the 5th century B.C., Nehemiah served as cupbearer to King Artaxerxes. Later, with the king's permission, he went back to Jerusalem to supervise construction of a wall around the city. Chapter 1 of Nehemiah tells us how he first heard of the plight of his people who were still in Jerusalem. The chapter goes on to describe his response to the news. By examining this slice of Nehemiah's life, we can uncover valuable insights about praying for others.

Read Nehemiah 1:1-11 carefully, and answer the following study questions:

1. What character qualities are reflected by Nehemiah's actions and words?

_____

_____

2. What is the relationship between character traits of this sort, and the ministry of intercession?

_____

_____

_____

_____

3. Scrutinize the content of his prayer (vss. 5-11). What observations or timeless principles concerning the act of intercession can you glean from his words?

_____

_____

_____

_____

_____

4. What impresses you most about the content of Nehemiah's prayer? Why?

_____

_____

_____

_____

_____

New Testament Examples

The New Testament is teeming with examples of intercession, and exhortations to become an intercessor. The following chart contains 7 references. Look up each reference, and jot down (by filling in the blanks) who was being prayed for, who did the praying, and the aim or purposes of the prayer (stated or implied). The first one is done for you.

Lk. 22:21-32

_____JESUS_____ prayed for _____SIMON_____.

Aim: _THAT HIS FAITH_
     WOULD NOT FAIL

Jn. 17:9-19

_____ prayed for _____.

Aim: _____

_____

Acts 12:5-12

_____ prayed for _____.

Aim: _____

_____

Ephesians 6:18-20

_____ prayed for _____.

Aim: _____

_____

Philippians 1:1-11

_____ prayed for _____.

Aim: _____

_____

Colossians 4:2-4

_____ prayed for _____.

Aim: _____

_____

II Timothy 1:1, 3

_____ prayed for _____.

Aim: _____

_____

Now answer the following questions regarding your completed prayer chart:

1. Which example of, or call to, intercession leaves the greatest impression on you? Why?

_____

_____

2. What conclusions about intercession can you draw from the things requested on behalf of others? (See the "Aim" sections of the chart.)

_____

_____

_____

_____

_____

3. Based on these references, ask the Lord to show you one specific application for your prayer life. Describe it here:

_____

_____

_____

Becoming an Intercessor

As an impetus for developing your practice of intercession, briefly interview three mature Christians before your group meets to go over this lesson. Explain the slant of this lesson, and that you've been instructed to interview three other believers. If it isn't feasible to arrange face-to-face appointments, feel free to use the phone. Ask them the following two questions and record the responses in the spaces provided.

1. For what reasons is intercession not a significant ministry for most Christians? (Put another way, what are some obstacles to a consistent life-style of interceding for others?)

_____

_____

_____

_____

2. What practical tips would you give someone who wants to pray more for others? (What are some down-to-earth ways to keep "I'll pray for you" from becoming a flippant cliché?)

_____

_____

_____

_____

Whoa . . . don't close your workbook yet. Before you get up for a cup of coffee or to put in another load of wash, personalize the input from the interviews.

3. The things that most often keep me from a more significant ministry of intercession are:

_____

_____

_____

4. One practical tip that can enhance my intercession and help me overcome those hindrances is:

_____

_____

_____

It is reasonable for me to reserve the following chunk of time each day for intercession:

_____

10

THE MINISTRY OF EVANGELISM

Back in college, I dated a girl named Noel. She attended a business school 30 miles from my campus. Most weekends we'd go out to dinner, see a movie, or play miniature golf. What enjoyable times we shared!

At least *I* was enjoying *her* company. But one evening I found out that I wasn't as important to her as I had thought. During graduation ceremonies at her college, I sat with Barbara—Noel's best friend since high school days. At the reception, as Barbara and I followed her around, Noel said good-bye to a circle of teachers. She excitedly introduced Barbara to every instructor. Not one failed to meet Barbara, to see the gleam in Noel's eyes as she chatted about her longtime friend. On the other hand, Noel introduced me to only one teacher. "Oh, yes. This is so-and-so from Wingate College," she blurted, almost apologetically. That evening was such a "downer" emotionally that I would have had to stretch on tiptoe in order to touch bottom!

True Love?

Reflecting on that embarrassing experience reminds me of a maxim about Christian living: *whether or not we introduce Christ to others is a great test of our true love for Him.* If Jesus is important to us, sharing Him with friends, co-workers, and relatives won't just come as an afterthought.

No matter what form it takes, our participation in evangelism puts us on the front line of God's work in the world. Personal outreach is both a privilege and a responsibility. Here's how Stuart Briscoe (in a speech to a group of college students) has explained the centrality of this ministry in God's work:

We have conditioned ourselves into thinking that all that really matters is that we should be good, honest, clean-living, churchgoing Christians. Now with all due respect, that's a cop-out. There are going to be souls in hell who are convinced you were a good, clean-living, churchgoing Christian, and they'll be in hell because they never heard that the Gospel is relevant to them.

Evangelism is not the added extra for those who are that-way inclined. The church is in the world's debt. I'm alarmed by the philosophy that the sole task of the church is to turn out nice Christian people. I believe the sole task of the church is to turn out people who honestly believe they have the only message of hope and that they are the only people who have it.

Whew! That should jar anyone loose from the grip of complacency! Let's explore some of the forms of witnessing, then concentrate on how to improve our verbal communication with non-Christians.

First Things First

When we see or hear the term "witness," we conjure up the image of a courtroom. We see a person called to testify in front of the judge and jury. The person is asked questions by the defendant's lawyer, or the prosecutor. The witness is called to testify because she supposedly has *evidence* regarding the guilt or innocence of the person on trial.

This courtroom analogy illustrates what the term means for Christians. To "witness" for Christ means *to furnish evidence of His reality.* We can give many different forms of evidence to persons in our spheres of influence. Our willingness to do so is a natural result of Christ living in us and channeling His life through us.

1. What does this definition of "witnessing" presuppose about your experience?

_____

_____

_____

2. Read II Corinthians 5:17-20. What is the relationship between verse 17 and verses 18-20?

_____

_____

_____

As the term "witness" implies, it's difficult to provide convincing evidence of something we haven't actually experienced. Only firsthand, _experiential_ knowledge qualifies us to take the witness stand for Christ. Though becoming a "new creation" (II Cor. 5:17) is a lifelong process, we can validly accept the "ministry of reconciliation" only when we ourselves have accepted Christ as Savior, and have been reconciled with God. We cannot manufacture the evidence of Christ's reality. Rather, it must be supernaturally produced by the indwelling Holy Spirit.

If you have received Christ as your Savior, keep reading. If not, your immediate need isn't to learn more about evangelism. Your need is to acknowledge that Jesus died on the cross for _your_ sins, and to personally invite Him into _your_ life. Only a personal relationship with Christ gives a witness credibility.

Word and Deed

There are two main ways to bear evidence: through _actions_, and through _verbal presentation_. Put simply, _actions_ are character qualities that show up in a changed pattern of behavior. As we grow in Christ, the way we relate to people, the motives for decisions we make, and the values we adopt fall in line with the commands and principles of Scripture. Gradually, non-Christians with whom we have regular contact will notice a difference. Some are attracted by the evidence of a changed life. On the other hand, *verbal evidence* includes informal sharing of what Christ has done for us, as well as a more systematic explanation of how an unbeliever can become a Christian (the "plan of salvation").

Right off the bat, let's hammer a fundamental principle into our minds: *Effective outreach to non-Christians involves a blend of Christlike actions and word-of-mouth testimony.* Conversing about the Lord, when divorced from a godly character and Biblical value system, repels genuine seekers. But merely living righteously, without occasional verbal explanations of the Gospel, may draw more attention to ourselves rather than Christ—and leave them wondering how they can get what we have.

Read the following sets of references and complete the sentences.

1. I Peter 2:9; 3:15; Psalm 145:1-7. The kind of evidence called for in these passages is:

_____

2. Colossians 3:1-17; Galatians 5:22, 23. The kind of evidence referred to here is:

_____

In his highly acclaimed book, *Lifestyle Evangelism*, Joe Aldrich emphasizes the need for evidence that is fleshed out in daily life:

Christians are to be good news before they share the good news. The words of the gospel are to be incarnated before they are verbalized. Let me put it another way. The music of the gospel must precede the words of the gospel and prepare the context in which there will be a hunger for those words.

What is the music of the gospel? The music of the gospel is the beauty of the indwelling Christ as lived out in the everyday relationships of life. The gospel is the good news that Jesus

Christ has solved the problem of man's sin and offers him the potential of an exchanged life, a life in which the resources of God Himself are available for his transformation. And as the gospel is translated into music, it makes redemptive relationships possible. When the world observes husbands loving their wives, and wives supporting and caring for their husbands and families, they have seen a miracle; they have heard the music. It is miraculous music for which many of them are longing. It's the old story: when love is seen, the message is heard.

Chances are, we all nod in agreement with Aldrich. Yet it's possible to swing the pendulum too far in the opposite direction—to live a godly life that reflects evidences of growth, without ever verbalizing the Gospel message to others. The Lord wants us to share with others what He has accomplished for us personally and to explain from Scripture how they can enter into a relationship with Him.

A college student, Jean, laments her silence in the face of witnessing opportunities: "I concentrated on living a good, silent life, hoping that through my actions alone friends would want to trust Christ. But they never brought up the subject of Jesus. They merely thought I was a 'do-gooder' since I refused to go along with some of their activities. Over a period of time our friendships weakened and they never knew I was trying to witness for Jesus through my actions. I learned that unless I verbalize the Gospel, my 'do-good' life tends only to draw attention to myself."

Let's Summarize

To sum up and apply what we've covered so far, answer the following questions.

1. The two ways to bear evidence of Christ's reality are:

_____

_____

2. One specific aspect of Christian character that I want to become more evident in my daily life-style is:

_____

_____

3. Read Hebrews 12:14. One way I can actively pursue the change described in #2 above is:

_____

_____

4. When I think of verbalizing my faith—sharing my personal testimony with non-Christians—I feel (circle words that apply):

scared stiff	a bit hesitant	raring to go!
unqualified	confident	like a failure

other: _____

I feel this way because (be specific!):

_____

_____

_____

_____

Learn to use the Bible to share God's plan of salvation—giving evidence *verbally*. The best verbal evidence conveys both personal history (sharing ways Jesus has changed us, answers to prayer, etc.), and Biblical truths that help others make a decision.

5. If an unbelieving acquaintance asked me, "How can I become a Christian?" I'd open my Bible and share with him or her the following truths and related Scripture verses: (Jot down what references and explanations you'd use to share God's plan of salvation with others.)

_____

_____

_____

_____

_____

_____

_____

If you feel inadequate verbalizing either your personal testimony or the claims of Christ from Scripture, don't feel all shot down. _The starting point of all growth is recognition of need._ Thank the Lord for exposing your need! The next meeting of your study group will offer practical tips and specific how-to helps for improving both aspects of your verbal witness.

Divine Resources

As you contemplate your involvement in evangelism, be encouraged—remember that it's a supernatural endeavor, and all the resources of God are at your disposal! We are merely channels of His power. He is the One who prepares hearts for our words, and effects a change in the unsaved.

Glance at Jesus' well-known Great Commission in Matthew 28:18-20. It's a mandate to get involved in the evangelism and discipleship of converts. What encouraging promise can you find in these verses? (It's a promise that can boost your confidence level when you witness.)

_____

_____

Now examine Acts 1:8. Based on these last earthly words of Jesus, what is the secret to power in witnessing?

_____

_____

The Holy Spirit indwells every believer, and we're dependent on His work every time we directly or indirectly involve ourselves in outreach. Specifically, how can we show our dependence on Him as we reach out with the Good News?

In high school, I had a crush on a cheerleader. For two years, I daydreamed about her and looked for her in crowded hallways. I told my pals how I felt about her, and occasionally I stuffed a mushy poem in her locker. Yet I didn't have the nerve to speak to her face-to-face. I figured she'd give me the brush-off. Then one afternoon I spotted her standing alone by her locker. I overcame wobbly knees, sweaty palms, and a racing heartbeat long enough to tell her how I felt. She stared at me for a few seconds, then asked wide eyed, "Why didn't you tell me this before?"

When they finally hear the Good News of Christ, many unbelievers must feel the same way. They have been in contact with Christians all their lives, but no one has taken the time to share with them the transforming message of Christ.

Right now, think of two or three non-Christian individuals for whom you're concerned (relatives, neighbors, co-workers, etc.). Put their names here:

Express your dependence on God's Spirit for their salvation by praying more consistently for these persons. Also, ask the Lord to show you concrete ways you can improve your relationship with each one, with the ultimate goal of verbally sharing your testimony with them. They may be more receptive to your actions and words than you think. Besides—the only failure in witnessing is silence.

11

PORTRAIT OF A USABLE PERSON

Most leaders or teachers have a list of goals for the particular group of people they serve. They work and pray for the Lord to move their people in a certain direction, spiritually speaking. Such goals are usually in harmony with God's desires for these people.

Think about an individual or group for whom you have some degree of spiritual responsibility (members of a Sunday school class you teach, participants in a club program or youth group that you lead, a person you're discipling, your children—anyone to whom you're ministering). Jot down the name or group here:

_____

Next, ponder this question: What are some characteristics that I want the Lord to develop in this person/group? List your answers below:

_____

_____

_____

_____

Godly Characteristics

Read I Thessalonians 1:1-10. Paul opens this letter to the believers in Thessalonica with thanksgiving for the life-changing work God had done in them. Go through this chapter and list the characteristics God had developed in a core group of Thessalonian believers:

_____

_____

_____

_____

_____

Put an asterisk beside the traits in I Thessalonians 1 that were also in your list of goals for your individual or group. Chances are, you want the Lord to create in your individual or group a teachable spirit in response to the Word; a deep-seated joy, even when the going is rough; and a witnessing life-style—things that marked the Thessalonian Christians.

God's Primary Method

But how does the Lord actually achieve those goals in the lives of our pupils, our disciples, and our children? How does He lead the people we serve into a deeper level of maturity?

To be sure, there is more than one valid answer to the "how" question. However, *God relies heavily on human leadership.* That is, God plans for the growth of others by exposing them to divinely gifted and appointed leaders: teachers, youth sponsors, club directors, parents—you name it! God develops certain characteristics in a person or group *by exposing them to us!*

This lesson spotlights the kind of person God uses. No matter what our spiritual gifts or ministry positions in the church, our true usefulness depends on allowing the Lord to nurture certain characteristics in us. This principle is vividly exhibited in I Thessalonians 1 and 2. Whereas chapter 1 contains qualities God was developing in the Thessalonians, chapter 2 describes the leaders responsible for such growth. After thanking God for evidences of growth (chap. 1), Paul begins to reminisce about his former ministry in Thessalonica (chap. 2). He reviews how he worked among them when the church was initially planted.

Now read I Thessalonians 2:1-20 slowly. Tucked away in these verses are answers to this study question: What personal qualities and ministry principles, modeled by Paul and his assistants, made them effective in Thessalonica? (Look for answers implied by Paul's words—not just those directly stated. Jot down your responses below. Pay close attention to specific words and phrases. Be analytical. Remember: you're looking for timeless secrets of usefulness to the Lord.)

_____

_____

_____

_____

_____

_____

1. Which characteristic or ministry insight do you feel is most essential for effective involvement in God's work in the 20th century? Why?

_____

_____

_____

2. Which attributes are most lacking among workers for God today? How do you explain this?

_____

_____

_____

3. Look over your list of leadership qualities and insights from I Thessalonians 2. Now review the characteristics that marked the Thessalonians, as seen in chapter 1. In what ways did the new Christians at Thessalonica "become like" Paul, their first leader?

_____

_____

_____

4. What ministry principle can you glean from your answer to the previous question? State it in one sentence:

_____

_____

Personalizing the Portrait

How do *you* compare to the portrait of an effective minister as seen in I Thessalonians 2? Reflect for a moment on your current leadership roles and/or ministry opportunities. Which two secrets of usefulness (found in I Thess. 2) do you want the Lord to develop in you?

_____

_____

Only God's Spirit can produce the desired changes. But we can choose whether or not to allow God to work in our lives. Think candidly for a moment. What do you need to change about your schedule or habits in order to tap God's resources for personal transformation?

_____

_____

No course on ministry involvement is complete without a proper perspective on usefulness. Bible knowledge and multiple talents are useless unless we nurture an ongoing relationship with the Lord, and make our personal growth a top priority. We can lead others only as far as we ourselves have come spiritually. Someone has put it this way: "In order to succeed in God's work, we frantically search for better methods and strategies. But God only looks for better people!"

In the next group meeting, your leader will help you apply the I Thessalonians 2 qualities to specific ministry tasks. As group members pool their insights on the passage, the portrait of an effective minister will crystallize even more.

12

USE IT
OR LOSE IT!

Every time I take a new course, attend a seminar, or read a book, his words come back to me. He spoke them over a decade ago, in an address to the student body at Wheaton College. But they often resurface, goading me into action. The moment I become slothful about what I've learned, or fail to convey to others what has benefited me, the statement echoes in my memory. What did pastor and author Stuart Briscoe say that holds me accountable?

God never blesses or teaches you solely for your own benefit.

It's all I remember from his hour-long message. But that sentence has been stamped deeply into my consciousness by God's Spirit, and it has transformed my ministry. I'm responsible to pass along to others what I'm learning. God intends for me to be a channel through which He educates others in the Body of Christ.

Looking Back

As you near the end of this *Welcome to Your Ministry* course, think about Briscoe's words in relation to what you've learned. You need to construct outlets so that whatever insights have flowed into your life over the past 12 weeks will eventually trickle out and refresh others as well. In this lesson you will review some of the things you've learned. You will also consider ways to multiply your investment in the course by conveying its content to others.

How humbling to realize that you are now more accountable to the Lord than you were before beginning the course!

Take several minutes to consider what you've gleaned from the weekly assignments in this workbook. Also, reflect on the supplementary insights provided by your study group leader, plus the spiritual benefits of interacting with other learners.

To refresh your memory, skim the various lesson titles and try to recall the main thrust of each lesson. As you look back, don't forget the practical ways you have applied the lessons, and the impact of God's Word on your attitudes and feelings.

1. One new insight about Christian living that I've reaped from this course is:

_____

_____

_____

2. The most threatening, hardest-hitting truth we've covered is:

_____

_____

_____

3. The one lesson or truth that has been most life changing for me is:

_____

_____

_____

4. One aspect of the group sessions that I've benefited most from is:

_____

_____

_____

5. Interspersed throughout the workbook and group sessions have been suggestions about how to communicate your learning to others (through teaching, discipling, letter writing, etc.). The most satisfying occasion in which I've communicated lesson content to others was:

_____

_____

Stewardship Plus

To have impact on others' lives with what you have learned in this course, you must realize that you are a *steward* of the material. In the New Testament, the term "steward" meant "one who manages a house for the owner." Of course, the term was applied figuratively to express all areas of accountability to God.

Crack open your Bible to I Corinthians 4:1-4.

1. What kind of "course management" does God expect? What word should describe a steward? (vs. 2)

_____

_____

2. To whom are we primarily accountable as stewards of what we've learned? (vss. 3, 4)

_____

Paul labeled himself a servant of "the secret things of God" (v. 1). The Greek word for "secret things" referred to insight or truth that had long been hidden, but was recently disclosed. Paul was alluding to the work of Christ, and the message of the cross. We, too, are stewards of the Gospel message. But our stewardship includes all new insights that God discloses to us as we grow in Christ—things previously a mystery (unknown) to us, but now crystallizing with time.

3. Look up Ephesians 5:15-17. What does this passage nudge us to manage carefully?

---

4. What reason does Paul give for managing our time on earth wisely?

Whether it is material wealth, time, natural abilities, spiritual gifts, experiences of God's faithfulness, or truth from His Word, we're expected to view what we possess as tools for ministry. Any other perspective warps God's intended purpose for blessing us in the first place. Now let's get more specific and probe a few ways to exercise stewardship of this course.

To Keep It—Give It Away!

Ironically, the more you give away the material you've learned in this course, the more you'll possess it. Your "ownership" of Scripture passages and principles for living increases each time you explain them to someone else. Communicating both requires you to concentrate on the concepts again, and enhances your retention of them.

Though suggestions for passing along material have been inserted within individual lessons, it's time to outline ways to transmit the course as a whole. If you aren't already implementing one of these suggestions, ponder these alternatives prayerfully:

ONE-ON-ONE DISCIPLESHIP. This approach is more informal, and doesn't require you to serve as a teacher in a public, technical sense. Possible settings include your living room, a restaurant, and your office. Your main resource is a completed *Welcome to Your Ministry* workbook. Of course, the person with whom you meet will need a new workbook.

Ask the Lord for the name of a person with whom to meet once a week for twelve weeks. A new believer who has an appetite for God's Word would make a good candidate. Put his or her name here _____ _____ . When you contact this individual, spell out the costs of the project (weekly assignments, willingness to apply lessons, etc.), and gauge the responsiveness.

Don't let your workbook gather dust on a shelf. The more wrinkled and dog-eared it becomes from use, the more impact you'll be having for the Kingdom of God.

HOME BIBLE STUDY. Invite two or three married couples (or four to six singles) into your home for 12 once-a-week sessions. Though this setting may require a bit more leadership than the one-on-one approach, it still doesn't call for the formal teaching expertise of a more structured classroom environment. Your main role will be to facilitate discussion of the completed assignments. If this approach entices you, ask your church for a copy of the **Leader's Guide** for the *Welcome to Your Ministry* course. Every participant will also need an individual workbook.

Think of persons in your church whom you want to know better, or neighbors and co-workers who may know the Lord, but who attend a church irregularly. Jot down the names of people whom you want to invite to this study venture:

_____

_____

_____

_____

_____

CHURCH-SPONSORED CLASS. Your church may want to offer this course again—especially if current learners promote it with word-of-mouth testimony of its benefits. If you feel that teaching is a gift God may have given you, and you're sold on the content of this course, offer to teach it the next time it's offered. Talk to your current group leader about the possibility. Ask for honest feedback on your potential as a teacher. You'll also need to investigate the formal approval processes required by your church for those in teaching positions.

Whether or not you teach it, two people you'd like to invite to this course the next time it's offered are:

_____

_____

"I'm willing to try my hand at teaching. But I'd feel more comfortable if I could receive training in the following areas":

_____

_____

_____

Businessmen constantly search for the secure investment, for one with a strong possibility of a high monetary yield. When you start sharing what you've learned with others, it will be an investment in eternity! Such a venture guarantees dividends, because you'll be investing in two "forever" entities: people, and the Word of God.

Which of the three alternatives is the most feasible investment opportunity for *you*? Go back and put a check mark (✔) beside the appropriate one.